Prayers That Avail Much®
for Young Adults

By Germaine Copeland

And this is the confidence that we have in him, that, if we ask anything according to his will, he heareth us: and if we know that he hear us, whatsoever we ask, we know that we have the petitions that we desired of him.

1 John 5:14,15

Harrison House LLC

Tulsa, Oklahoma

D1432843

17 16 15 14 13   10 9 8 7 6 5 4 3 2 1

Prayers That Avail Much for Young Adults
ISBN: 978-160683-693-4
Copyright © 2013 by Germaine Copeland
P. O. Box 289
Good Hope, Georgia 30641

Published by Harrison House Publishers
P.O. Box 35035
Tulsa, Oklahoma 74153
www.harrisonhouse.com

Presented to

By

Date

Occasion

Contents

Special Prayers

A Word from the Author:

The prayers in this book have the power to take you into your future! Do not simply read, but speak the scriptural prayers to the Father. He isn't in a far-away place; He is as close as your breath.

Whether you pray an entire prayer, one sentence or a paragraph, you are hiding God's Word in your heart. These scriptural prayers will teach you what is right and honest and fair; you will gain knowledge and wisdom.

Take time to read the book of Proverbs, which gives you practical insight for everyday living. At school and/or at work, expect to find favor and good understanding with God and with man.

You could have been born in another lifetime, but the Creator of the universe chose you for this present generation. It is my prayer that you will be ever learning, ever growing and ever achieving to the glory of God.

Remember you have a friend who is praying for you!

Germaine

Part I:

Daily Prayers

Beginning Each Day

Father, today belongs to You! I will celebrate and be glad wherever I may be. It is better to obey than to sacrifice so I submit to Your will so that my plans and purposes may be conducted in a manner that will bring honor and glory to You. Thank You for keeping me spiritually and mentally alert in this time of meditation and prayer.

I completely trust You and place myself and those for whom I pray in your keeping knowing You are able to guard everything and everyone that I entrust to You. Thank You for ordering Your angels to protect me, my family and friends. They will hold us up with their hands so that we won't even hurt our feet on a stone. Thank You, Father that Your love never ends and Your mercy never stops. Your loyalty to me is awesome!

Father, I kneel in prayer to You. You are wonderful and glorious. I pray that Your Spirit will make me a strong follower and that Christ will live in my heart because of my faith.

You can do anything, Father – far more than I could ever imagine or guess or request in my wildest dreams by Your Spirit within me. Glory to You forever! Amen.

Scripture References

Psalm 118:24 CEV

2 Timothy 1:12 NLT

Lamentations 3:22-23 NCV

Ephesians 3:20 MSG

1 Samuel 15:22 NCV

Psalm 91:11-12 NLT

Ephesians 3:14-17 CEV

Trust in the Lord

Father, You are my God. I worship You with all my heart; I long for You just as I would long for a stream in a desert. I know that You hear me when I call to You for help. You rescue me from all my troubles. Many are against me, but You keep me safe. You give me the victory! I depend on You and I have chosen to trust You since I first believed. I can be sure that You will protect me from harm. In Christ, I have been made right with God and my prayers have great power and produce wonderful results!

Jesus is the High Priest of my faith. I am completely free to enter the Most Holy Place without fear because of the blood of the Lamb. I can enter through a new and living way that Jesus opened for me. I am confident that You hear me whenever I ask for anything that pleases You. And since I know that

You hear me when I make my requests, I also know that You will give me what I ask for.

In the moment that I get tired in the waiting, Holy Spirit, You are right alongside, helping me along. If I don't know how or what to pray, You help me pray, making prayer out of my wordless sighs and my aching groans. You know me far better than I know myself. This is why I can be so sure that every detail in my life is worked into something good.

In the name of Jesus, I will keep on being brave. I know it will bring me great rewards. I will learn to be patient so that I will please You, Lord, and receive what You have promised. I live by faith in the Son of God who loved me and gave Himself to save me. Hallelujah! Praise You Lord!

Scripture References

Psalm 63:1 CEV	Hebrews 3:1 NCV
Psalm 34:17 NLT	Hebrews 10:19-25 NCV

Psalm 55:17,18 NCV

Psalm 71:5 CEV

Proverbs 3:26 CEV

Hebrews 10:35,36 CEV

Galatians 2:20 NIV

1 John 5:14,15 NLT

Romans 8:26-28 MSG

1 Corinthians 1:30 NCV

James 5:16 NLT

Watch What You Say

Father, today I determine with Your help to let everything I say be good and helpful, so that my words will be an encouragement to those who hear them. I turn from evil talk and foolish speaking, instead giving thanks to God. I stay away from useless talk and pointless discussions knowing that those things lead people further away from You.

Your Word says the tongue is a flame of fire—a whole world of wickedness, corrupting the entire body. In the name of Jesus, I make every effort to control my tongue, which allows me to control myself in every other way. I use godly wisdom to make knowledge acceptable to others. I have trustworthy things to say and I speak what is right. I detest lying.

Because I have been made right with God through Christ, I set the course of my life for obedience, abundance, wisdom, health, and joy. Lord, put a watch over my mouth, keep watch over the door of my lips. Then I will tell of Your goodness; I will speak of Your salvation. I realize that I keep my soul from trouble by watching over my mouth.

Father, Your words are top priority to me. They are spirit and life. I let Christ's words with all their wisdom and richness live in me. I believe Your Word and I speak Your Word—it is alive and powerful in me. My words are words of faith, power, love, and life. They bring good things to my life and to the lives of others as I come to know every blessing I have in Christ Jesus. Amen.

Scripture References

Ephesians 4:29 NCV

Ephesians 5:4 CEV

2 Timothy 2:16 CEV

James 3:6 NIV
NKJV

John 10:10 NIV

Psalm 141:3 NLT

Psalm 71:15 NKJV

Proverbs 21:23

James 3:2 NIV

Proverbs 15:2 CEV

Proverbs 8:6-7 CEV

2 Corinthians 5:21 NIV

Proverbs 4:23 NIV

John 6:63 NIV

Colossians 3:16 GW

Hebrews 4:12 GW

2 Corinthians 4:13 NIV

Philemon 1:6 NCV

God's Wisdom and Will

Lord, You are worthy to receive glory and honor and power. You created all things and by Your will they were created and have their being. You adopted me as Your child through Jesus Christ, in accordance with Your pleasure and will. As I share the faith I have in common with others, I pray that I may come to have a complete knowledge of all the good things I have in Christ.

Father, I ask You to fill me with a knowledge of Your will through all the wisdom and understanding that the Spirit gives so that I will live a life worthy of You, Lord, and please You in every way. Let my life bear fruit in every good work, as I grow in the knowledge of God.

I roll my works upon You, Lord, and You make my thoughts agreeable to Your will, so my plans are established and succeed. You direct my steps and make them sure. I will not act thoughtlessly but will learn what You want me to do. I pray that I will stand firm in all the will of God, mature and fully assured.

Father, You have chosen me and make Your will known to me. Thank You, Holy Spirit, for leading me into all truth and telling me of things to come. God's Spirit and my spirit are in open communion. I am spiritually alive and have access to everything God's Spirit is doing. Christ knows what God is doing and I have His Spirit.

Father, I'm glad to have entered into Your rest and ceased from the weariness and pain of human labors, in Jesus' name, Amen.

Scripture References

Revelation 4:11 NIV	Colossians 4:12 NIV
Ephesians 1:5 NIV	Acts 22:14 WE
Philemon 1:6 GW	John 16:13 NLV

Colossians 1:9-10 NIV

Proverbs 16:3, 9 AMP

Ephesians 5:17 NCV

1 Corinthians 2:16 MSG

Hebrews 4:10 AMP

Health and Healing

Father, Your Word promises healing for Your children and I come before You asking You to remember Your promise in my life. It is written that prayer that comes from faith will heal the sick, for You will restore them to health. And if they have sinned, they will be forgiven. Right now, I let go of all unforgiveness, resentment, anger, and bad feelings toward anyone.

My body is the temple of the Holy Spirit who lives in me and I desire to be in good health. I seek truth that will make me free—both spiritually and naturally (good eating habits, medications if necessary, and appropriate rest and exercise). You bought me with a high price, and I desire to honor You with my body and spirit—they both belong to You.

Thank You, Father, for sending Your Word to heal

me and deliver me from all my destructions. Jesus, You are the Word who became human and lived among us. You took on Yourself my troubles (sickness, weakness, and distresses) and carried my sorrows and pains. You were hurt for my wrong-doing. You were crushed for my sins. You were punished so I would have peace. You were beaten so I would be healed and made whole.

Father, I pay attention to what You say and listen carefully to Your words. I will not lose site of them. I let them penetrate deep into my heart, for they bring life and healing to my whole body. You forgive my sins, heal all my diseases, redeem me from death, crown me with love and tender mercies, and fill my life with good things. My youth is renewed like the eagles!

The Spirit of God, who raised Jesus from the dead, lives in me. And just as God raised Christ from the dead, He will give life to my mortal body by this same Spirit living within me. Thank You that I will prosper in all things and be in health, even as my soul prospers.

In the name of Jesus, amen.

Scripture References

James 5:15 CEB

1 Corinthians 6:19-20 NLT

John 8:32 NCV

Psalm 107:20 NKJV

John 1:14 NCV

Isaiah 53:4-5 NLV

Proverbs 4:20-22 NLT

Psalm 103:3-5 NLT

Romans 8:11 NLT

3 John 2 NKJV

Setting of Proper Priorities

Father, too often I waste my time on useless, mere busywork and I am asking You to help me establish the correct priorities in my work. I confess my weakness of procrastination and lack of organization. I want to use my head and make the most of every chance that I get!

You have given me a seven-day week – six days to work and the seventh day to rest. I want to make the most of every day that You have given me. Help me to plan my time and stay focused on my assignments.

In the name of Jesus, I break down every big idea that tries to stop people from knowing God. I take every thought prisoner to make it obey You, Lord. I want to live a life of obedience to You.

Lord, You are the One who makes my plans succeed. I plan my way, but You direct my steps and make them sure. I trust You to help me organize my efforts, schedule my activities and budget my time.

Jesus, You want me to relax. You will show me how to take a real rest and learn the unforced rhythms of grace. If I keep company with You, I will learn to live freely and lightly.

By the grace given to me, I will not worry about missing out, and my everyday human concerns will be met. I will work first for Your kingdom, do what You call good and then I will have all the other things I need.

Father, through You I have a full and true life. I give all my worries and cares to You because You care about me. At the same time, I will stay alert and watch out for the enemy, the devil.

I cry out for insight and raise my voice for understanding. I make insight my priority!

Father, You sent Jesus that I might live and enjoy life to the full. Help me remember that my relationships with You and with others are more important than anything else. Amen.

Scripture References

Ephesians 5:15-16 MSG	Genesis 2:2 NIV
2 Corinthians 10:5-6 WE	Proverbs 16:3,9 AMP
Matthew 11:29 MSG	Colossians 2:10 NCV
Matthew 6:33 WE	1 Peter 5:7-8 NLT
Proverbs 2:3 AMP	John 10:10 WE

*If you do not know your strengths and weaknesses, ask the Holy Spirit to reveal them to you. The Lord speaks to us: "My grace is sufficient for you, for power is perfected in weakness" (2 Cor. 12:9 NASB).

Part II:

Personal Prayers

Glorify God

Because of God's loving kindness to me, I worship Him with my whole being. I let my body be a living and holy gift to Him. He is pleased with this gift of true worship. God is working in me, giving me the desire and the power to do what pleases Him.

Father, since I am right with You, I will live by faith. I refuse to turn back with fear, for that would not please You. My body is the temple of the Holy Spirit who lives in me. I don't belong to myself. Lord, You bought me with a high price and I honor You with my body.

I call on You in times of trouble; You save me, and I honor You. For you have rescued me from the dominion of darkness and brought me into the Kingdom of the Son You love. With all my heart I will praise You, my Lord and my God. I will give glory to Your name forever!

Thank You Lord for the talents You have given me. I want You to say of me, "Well done, good and faithful servant." I will make good use of the gifts given to me by Your grace. I will be a light for other people. I will live so they will see the good things I do give praise to You.

In Jesus' name, I will speak the truth in love, growing in every way more and more like Christ. Everything I say or do, I will do in the name of Jesus, giving thanks to You, God, my Father. In all the work I do, I will do the best I can. I will work as if I were doing it for the Lord and not for people. Amen.

Salvation

Father, it is written in Your Word that if I declare with my mouth, "Jesus is Lord" and if I believe in my heart that You raised Him from the dead, then I will be saved. So, I declare with my mouth that Jesus is my Lord. I make Him Lord of my life right now. I believe in my heart that You raised Jesus from the dead. I am putting my past life behind me and I close the door to Satan and any of his devices.

I thank You for forgiving me of all my sin. Jesus is my Lord and I am a new person. The old things have passed away and now all things have become new in Jesus' name. Amen.

Scripture Reference

John 3:16	John 14:6
John 6:37	Romans 10:9,10 NLT
John 10:10b	Romans 10:13

Romans 3:23

2 Corinthians 5:19

John 16:8,9

Romans 5:8

Ephesians 2:1-10 NCV

2 Corinthians 5:17

John 1:12

2 Corinthians 5:21

To Receive the Infilling of the Holy Spirit

Father, I am Your child because I believe in my heart that Jesus has been raised from the dead and I have declared with my mouth that He is my Lord.

Jesus said that the Heavenly Father is ready to give the Holy Spirit to anyone who asks. I ask You now in the name of Jesus to fill me with the Holy Spirit. I step into the fullness and power that I desire in the name of Jesus.

Scripture Reference

John 14:16,17	Acts 10:44-46
Luke 11:13 NLT	Acts 19:2,5,6
Acts 1:8a	1 Corinthians 14:2-15

Scripture References

Romans 12:1 NLV	Matthew 25:21 NKJV

Philippians 2:13 NLT

Hebrews 10:38 NCV

1 Corinthians 6:20 NLT

Psalm 50:15 NCV

Colossians 1:13 NIV

Psalm 86:12 NLT

Acts 2:4

Acts 2:32,33,39

Acts 8:12-17

Romans 12:6 NIV

Matthew 5:16 NCV

Ephesians 4:15 NLT

Colossians 3:17 GW

Colossians 3:23 NIV

Jude 1:20

1 Corinthians 14:18,27

Ephesians 6:18

Boldness

Father, in the name of Jesus, I ask You to give me the courage to speak Your Word with great boldness. When the Holy Spirit came upon me, I received the power to be Your witness. I will tell people about You everywhere. Thank You for giving me this wonderful message of reconciliation that You are no longer counting people's sins agasinst them. I pray for right words to speak so I can make known the mystery of the Gospel for which I am an ambassador of Jesus Christ. God, You make Your appeal through me, and I speak for You when I plead, "Come back to God!"

I take comfort and am encouraged and confidently and boldly say, "The Lord is my Helper; I will not be seized with alarm—I will not fear or dread or be terrified. What can man do to me?" Father God, You made Christ, who never sinned, to be the offering for my sin so that I am made right with You through Christ. I am complete in Him, righteous, and as bold as a lion, in Jesus name, amen.

Scripture References

2 Corinthians 5:19-21 NLT   Hebrews 13:6 AMP

Forgiveness

Father, in the name of Jesus I make a fresh commitment to You to live in peace – to get along with everybody – with my brothers and sisters of the Body of Christ, with my friends, associates, neighbors, and family.

Father, I repent of holding on to bad feelings toward others. Today I let go of bitterness, rage, anger, harsh words and slander, and all other types of bad behavior. I ask Your forgiveness for the sin of _____. By faith, I receive Your forgiveness knowing that You cleanse me from all the wrongs that I have done. I ask You to forgive and release all who have wronged and hurt me. In the name of Jesus, I forgive and release them, and will show them kindness and mercy just as You have shown me.

From this moment on, I give up my evil ways, and will be gentle and sensitive to others speaking kind

words of encouragement, and I will do what is right.
I know that I have right-standing with You, Father
and You watch over everyone who obeys You and You
listen to my prayers.

Thank You for Your love that has been poured
into my heart by the Holy Spirit who is given to me. I
believe that love touches everyone I know. Then all of
us will be filled with the fruit of our salvation – which
is the righteous character produced in our lives by
Christ Jesus. So be it! Amen.

Scripture References

Romans 12:16-18 MSG

Romans 12:10

Philippians 2:2

Ephesians 4:31 NLT

Ephesians 4:27

Philippians 1:9,11 NLT

Mark 11:25

Ephesians 4:32 CEV

1 Peter 3:8,11,12 CEV

Colossians 1:10

Romans 5:5

Holiness

Thank You Father for making me holy by Your truth; You teach me Your Word, which is truth. Jesus, You gave Yourself as a holy sacrifice for me so I can be made holy by Your truth. Father, in Jesus' name, I confess my sins to You and You are faithful and just to forgive me my sins and to cleanse me from all wickedness.

You live in me and walk with me—You are my God and I am Your child. So I leave the corruption and compromise; I leave it for good. You are my Father, and I will not link up with those who would pollute me, because You want me all for Yourself. I make myself pure—free from anything that makes body or soul unclean. I will try to become holy in the way I live because I respect God.

I throw off my old sinful nature and former way of life. I let the Spirit renew my thoughts and at-

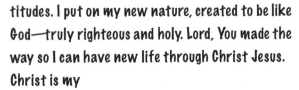

titudes. I put on my new nature, created to be like God—truly righteous and holy. Lord, You made the way so I can have new life through Christ Jesus. Christ is my

wisdom. Christ made me right with You. Now I am set apart for You and made holy. Christ bought me with His blood and made me free from sin.

I turn from evil and learn to do good, to seek justice, and help the oppressed. All who make themselves clean from evil will be used for noble purposes. I am made holy, useful to the Master, and ready to do any good work.

Thank you, Lord, that I eat the best from the land, because You have given me a willing and obedient heart. Amen.

Scripture References

John 17:17, 19 NLT

1 John 1:9 NLT

Ephesians 4:22-24 NLT

1 Corinthians 1:30 NLT

2 Corinthians 6:16 NCV

2 Corinthians 6:17 MSG

2 Corinthians 7:1 NCV

Isaiah 1:16-17 NLT

2 Timothy 2:21 NIV

Isaiah 1:19 GW

Love

Father, in Jesus name, I thank You that You fill my heart with love by the Holy Spirit which has been given to me. I keep and treasure Your Word. Your love and my love for You has truly reached its goal in me; and that true love chases all my worries away.

Father, I am Your child and I commit to walk in the God-kind of love. I will never give up. I care more for others than myself. I don't strut. I don't want what I don't have. I don't force myself on others or think about me first. I don't fly off the handle. I don't keep score of others' sins. I don't revel when others grovel but I take pleasure in the flowering of truth. I put up with anything. I trust God always. I always look for the best, never looking back; I keep going until the end. The love of God in me never dies.

Father, I bless and pray for those who would

harm me. I wish them well and do not curse them.
Because of this, my love will overflow more and more
in knowledge and understanding. I will live a pure and
blameless life until the day of Christ's return. I am
filled with the fruits of righteousness – the righteous
character produced in my life by Christ Jesus.

Everywhere I go, I commit to plant seeds of love.
I thank You, Father for preparing hearts ahead of
time to receive this love. I know that these seeds will
produce Your love in the hearts of those to whom they
are given.

Father, I thank You that as I walk in Your love and
wisdom, people are being blessed by my life and ministry. Father, You make me to find favor, respect and
affection with others (name them).

My life is strong and built on love. I know that
You are on my side and nothing is able to separate
me from Your love, Father which is in Christ Jesus

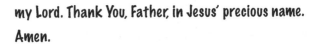

my Lord. Thank You, Father, in Jesus' precious name.
Amen.

Scripture References

Romans 5:5

1 John 2:5 NCV

1 John 4:18 CEV

1 Corinthians 3:6

Romans 12:14 NCV

Matthew 5:44

Philippians 1:9-11 NLT

John 13:34

1 Corinthians 13:4-8 MSG

Daniel 1:9 NLT

Ephesians 3:17 NCV

Romans 8:31,39

Safety

Father, in the name of Jesus, I lift my family up to You and pray a wall of protection around us – our home and property. Father, You are a wall of fire around us and You have sent Your angels to protect us.

I thank You that we live under the protection of God Most High and we stay in the shadow of God All-Powerful. We will say to You, Lord, that You are our fortress, our place of safety. You are our God and we trust You! You will cover us with Your feathers and hide us under Your wings. We will not fear any danger by night or an arrow during the day. We will watch and see the sinful punished.

You are our fortress and we run to You for safety. Because of this, no terrible disasters will strike us or our home. You will command Your angels to protects us wherever we go. You have said in Your Word that

You will save whoever loves You. You will protect
those who know You. You will be with us in trouble.
You will rescue us and honor us and give us a long,
full life and show us Your salvation. Not a hair of our
head will perish.

Thank You, Father, for Your watch, care, and protection over my family and me. In Jesus' name. Amen.

Scripture References

Job 1:10 NLT

Zechariah 2:5

Psalm 34:7 CEV

Psalm 91:1, 2 CEV

Psalm 91:4,5 NCV

Psalm 91:8 NCV

Psalm 9:9-11 CEV

Psalm 91:14-16 NCV

Luke 21:18 NIV

Worry Free

Father, thank You that I have been rescued from the dominion of darkness and brought into the Kingdom of the Son You love. I loose the feeling of anxiety from my emotions, and determine to live free from worry in the name of Jesus, for the law of the Spirit of life in Christ Jesus has made me free from the law of sin and death.

I humble myself under Your mighty power and at the right time, You will lift me up in honor. I give all my worries and cares to You, for You care about me. I pile all my troubles on Your shoulders. Thank You for carrying my load and helping me out. You'll never let me fall into ruin. Father, I take delight in You, and You perfect that which concerns me.

I break down every thought and proud thing that puts itself up against the wisdom of God. I take hold of every thought and make it obey Christ. I rid myself of everything that gets in the way and the sin that tries to hold on to me so tightly. I run with determination the race that lies before me, keeping my eyes fixed on Jesus, on whom my faith depends from beginning to end.

I know the One in whom I trust and I am sure that You are able to guard what I have entrusted to You until the day of Your return. I fix my thoughts on what is true, honorable, right, pure, lovely, and admirable. I think about things that are excellent and worthy of praise. I will not let my heart be troubled. I live in You and Your words remain in me and live in my heart. I do not forget what manner of person I am. I look into the perfect law that sets me free; I do what it says; I do not forget what I have heard and God blesses me for doing it.

Thank You, Father. I refuse to worry about anything; instead, I pray about everything and the peace of God which transcends all understanding guards my heart and mind in Christ Jesus. Amen.

Scripture References

Colossians 1:13 NIV

Romans 8:2 NKJV

1 Peter 5:6-7 NLT

Psalm 55:22 MSG

Psalm 37:4 NIV

Psalm 138:8 NKJV

2 Corinthians 10:5 NLV

Hebrews 12:1,2 GNT

2 Timothy 1:12 NLT

Philippians 4:8 NLT

John 14:1 NIV

John 15:7 AMP

James 1:22-25 NLT

Philippians 4:6 NLT

NOTE: Worrying may be one of the most common temptations. It often presents itself in an innocent package. Immediately, upon becoming aware of this insidious, sinful practice, I begin quoting Scripture, which has proven to be a most effective weapon!

Success in Christ

Thank You Father that the teaching of Your Word gives light. The Word You speak (and I speak) is alive and full of power—making it active, operative, energizing, and effective. I receive the spirit of power and of love and of a calm and well-balanced mind and discipline and self-control that You have given to me. My qualification comes from You, and You have enabled me to be a minister of Your New Covenant—not of written laws but of the Spirit, who gives life.

In the name of Jesus, I submit to the destiny You planned for me before the foundation of the world. I give thanks to You, Father, for qualifying me to share in the inheritance of Your holy people in the Kingdom of Light. Father, thank You for showing me that every "failure" is a learning experience and another stepping stone to success.

You rescued me from the dominion of darkness

(failure, doubt, and fear) and brought me into the Kingdom of the Son You love. I study and remember Your teachings and it makes me wise and successful. My joy is in Jesus who has come that I may have life and have it more abundantly.

I belong to Christ and I am a new person. The old life is gone and a new life has begun. The past no longer controls my decisions; I forget the things that are behind and look forward to what lies ahead. I have been crucified with Christ and I no longer live, but Christ lives in me. The life I now live in the body, I live by faith in the Son of God, who loved me and gave Himself for me.

Today I listen carefully to God's words. I don't lose sight of them. I let them penetrate deep into my heart, for they bring life to me and healing to my whole body. I guard my heart above all else, for it determines the course of my life.

Today I hold onto kindness and truth. I tie them around my neck and write them upon my heart. So I will find favor and good understanding in the eyes of God and man.

Today my delight is in the teachings of the Lord and I reflect on them day and night. So I am like a tree planted beside streams—a tree that produces fruit in season and whose leaves do not wither. I succeed in everything I do.

Thank You Father for the power Christ has given me. He leads me and makes me win in everything, amen.

Scripture References

Psalm 1 1 9:1 30 NLT	2 Corinthians 5:17 NLT
Hebrews 4:1 2 AMP	Philippians 3:1 3 NLT
2 Timothy 1:7 AMP	Galatians 2:20 NIV
2 Corinthians 3:5-6 NLT	Proverbs 4:20-23 NLT
Colossians 1:1 2-1 3 NIV	Proverbs 3:3-4 NLV

Joshua 1:8 NCV

John 10:10 NKJV

Psalm 1:2-3 GW

2 Corinthians 2:14 NLV

Before a Vacation or Roadtrip

Father, today, in Jesus' name, I speak Your words over my travel plans knowing that Your words do not return empty, but they make things happen that You want to happen and they succeed in doing what You send them to do. Thank You for watching to make sure Your words come true.

As I prepare to travel, I remember it is You alone, Lord, who keeps me safe. I live under the protection of God Most High. If I face any problems or trouble, You are a mighty tower that I can run to for safety. My trust is in the Lord and I am safe. Believing in the written Word of God, I speak peace, safety, and success over my travel plans.

As Your child, my path of travel is guarded by You and my life is protected. You order Your angels to protect me wherever I go. I will proceed with my travel plans without fear of accidents, problems, or any type of frustrations—You have given me a calm, well-balanced mind. I have Your peace and it guards my heart and mind as I live in Christ Jesus. Thank You, Father, that in every situation, You are there to protect me. No matter in what means of transportation I choose to travel, You will protect me. You are my Heavenly Father and I am Yours. Through my faith in You, I have the power to trample on snakes and scorpions and to overcome all the power of the enemy—nothing will harm me. Even if I were to contact something poisonous, it will not hurt me. In fact, I'm able to place my hands on the sick and they will be healed.

Whatever I forbid on earth will be forbidden in heaven and whatever I permit on earth will be permitted in heaven. I can ask for anything in the name of Jesus and He will do it, so that the Son can bring glory to the Father. (Asking in the name of Jesus indicates I am asking in agreement with His will.)

Father, I honor You and Your mercy is upon me and my family, and our travels will be safe. Thank You for Your guidance and safety—You are worthy of all praise, amen.

Scripture References

Isaiah 55:1 1 NCV

Jeremiah 1:1 2 NCV

Psalm 4:8 NLT

Psalm 91:1 CEV

Proverbs 18:1 0 CEV

Proverbs 29:25 GW

Mark 11:23-24 NIV

Proverbs 2:8 NLT

Psalm 91:1 1-12 NLT

2 Timothy 1:7 AMP

Philippians 4:7 NLT

2 Timothy 4:1 8 NIV

Isaiah 43:1-3 NCV

Luke 10:1 9 NIV

Psalm 91:1 3 CEV

Mark 16:1 8 NLT

Matthew 18:1 8 NLT

John 14:1 3 NLT

Daniel 9:1 8 NIV

Luke 1:50 GNT

Luke 21:1 8 NIV

Peaceful Sleep

Father, thank You for peaceful sleep and for Your angels that protect us. Praise the Lord for angels who are mighty and carry out Your plans. They listen for Your instructions and obey Your voice. You command Your angels to protect us wherever we go.

We capture every thought and make it obey You, Father. I thank You that Your Word says that we can go to bed without fear and we can lie down and sleep soundly. Praise You, Lord for being our guide. Even in the darkest night, we feel Your leading. We will always look to You as You stay close beside us and protect us from fear. With all of our hearts, we rejoice and are glad that we can safely rest. You give sleep to Your children. Thank You, Father, that we can sleep soundly because You keep us safe!

Scripture References

Psalm 34:7 CEV

Psalm 103:20 NCV & NLT

Psalm 91:11 CEV

2 Corinthians 10:5 NCV

Proverbs 3:24 NLT

Psalm 16:7-9 CEV

Psalm 127:2 NCV

Psalm 4:8

Committing to a Life of Purity

Father, I come before Your throne of grace in the name of Jesus. In the past I lived the way the world lives, doing all the things my body and mind wanted to do.

But, God—Your mercy is great! Even though I was spiritually dead, You loved me so much that You gave me a new life with Christ. I have been saved by Your grace and raised up with Christ, seated with Him in the heavens.

You are my Father, and I belong to You. Since I am in Christ, I have become a new person. My old life is gone and my new life has begun. Therefore, I rid myself of all malice, deceit, hypocrisy, envy, and slander of every kind. Like a newborn baby, I crave pure spiritual milk, so that I may grow up in Your salvation.

I submit myself to Jesus Christ, who loves me and

sacrificed His life for me to make me holy, cleansing me through the baptism of His Word. I am now radiant in Your eyes—free from spot, wrinkle, and any other blemish—I am holy and without guilt.

Thank You for the blood of Christ that cleans me inside and out. Through the Spirit, Christ became an unblemished sacrifice for me, freeing me from all the dead-end efforts to make myself respectable, so that I can live all out for You! Thank You for giving me the Holy Spirit, who is holy and pure.

I ask for and receive wisdom, which comes from heaven—it is first of all pure; it is also peace loving, gentle at all times, willing to yield to others, full of mercy and good deeds, shows no favoritism, and is always sincere. Change my impure language, Lord, and give me clear and pure speech so that it is pleasing to You.

I purpose not to conform to the ways of this world, but I am transformed by the renewing of my mind, and I take every thought captive to the obedience of Christ. I fix my thoughts on whatever is true, noble, right, pure, lovely, and admirable. I determine to think on things that are excellent or praiseworthy. I am careful what I think on, because thoughts run our lives.

What marvelous love You have extended to me, that I am now called and counted as a child of God! Father, I have no idea where I'll end up, but I do know that when You are openly revealed, I will see You and will become like You.

Because of the blood of the Lamb and the word of my testimony, I will overcome. In Jesus' name I pray, amen.

Scripture References

Ephesians 2:2-6 NCV

2 Corinthians 5:17 NLT

1 Peter 2:1,2 NIV

Proverbs 15:16 NCV

Zephaniah 3:9 NLT

Romans 12:2 NIV

Philippians 4:8 NIV

Proverbs 4:23 NCV

James 3:17 NLT

2 Corinthians 10:5 NASB

Ephesians 5:25-27 Phillips

1 Thessalonians 4:8 NASB

Hebrews 9:14 MSG

1 John 3:1-3 MSG

Revelation 12:11 NASB

Psalm 101:3 AMP

Employment

Father, _____ needs employment; a job where Your abundant supply is released to his/her good and benefit.

Father, I believe and confess Your Word over _____, knowing that every word You give comes true. Your words do not return to You empty, but succeed in doing what You sent them to do. Father, You are his/her source of all comfort and encouragement and he/she is strong and courageous, standing firm in the faith.

_____'s desire is to owe no man anything except love. Therefore, he/she is strong and does not let his/her hands be lazy because he/she knows that payday is coming. His/her pay is not given as a gift, but as something earned. _____ makes it his/her goal to live a quiet life, working with his/her hands so that he/she

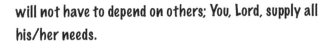
will not have to depend on others; You, Lord, supply all his/her needs.

He/She works quietly and earns his/her own food and other necessities and does not tire of doing good. _____ maintains good works – honest labor and honorable employment – so that he/she may be fruitful.

Father, because _____ has obeyed Your Word, You have opened a door for him/her that no one can shut.

_____ is not afraid or discouraged because he/she knows You are God, and You will always be with him/her. You give him/her strength and hold him/her in Your victorious right hand. In the name of Jesus, I loose worry and fretting from his/her mind. He/She brings his/her concerns to You and You give him/her peace and wholeness, displacing the worry at the center of his/her life.

_____ guards his/her mouth and tongue, keeping himself/herself out of trouble.

_____ prizes wisdom and acknowledges You and You make his/her paths straight and promote him/her. Therefore, he/she increases in wisdom and in favor with You and with man. In Jesus' name, amen.

Scripture References

Jeremiah 1:12 MSG

Isaiah 55:11 NCV

2 Corinthians 1:3 NLT

1 Corinthians 16:13 NIV

Romans 13:8 NASB

2 Chronicles 15:7 MSG

Romans 4:4 NCV

1 Thessalonians 4:11,12 NLT

2 Thessalonians 3:12,13 NCV

Luke 2:52 NIV

Titus 3:14 ASV

Revelation 3:8 WE

Isaiah 41:10 NLT

John 16:33 WE

Philippians 4:6,7 MSG

Philippians 4:12,13 NASB

Proverbs 21:23 NIV

Proverbs 3:6 NASB

Proverbs 4:8 AMP

Choosing Godly Friends

Father, help me to show myself friendly and meet new friends. I want to spend time with wise people so that I may become wise by learning from them. I know that You are my source of love, companionship and friendship. Help me to express and receive Your love and friendship with members of the body of Christ.

Just as iron sharpens iron, friends sharpen each other. As we learn from each other, may we share the same love and have one mind and purpose. Help me, Lord to be well-balanced in my friendships so that I will always please You rather than others.

Lord, I ask for divine connections and good friendships and thank You for the courage and grace to let go of detrimental friendships. I ask for Your discernment for developing healthy relationships. Your Word says that two people are better than one because if one person falls, the other can reach out and help.

Father, only You know the hearts of people so help me to discern and not be deceived by outward appearances. Thank You, Lord that every good and perfect gift comes from You and I thank You for quality friends. Help me to be a friend to others and love at all times. When others are happy, I will be happy with them. When they are sad, I will be sad with them. Help me to learn how to be a responsible and reliable friend.

Develop in me a fun personality and a good sense of humor. Help me to relax around people and be myself – the person You created me to be. I want to be a faithful and trustworthy friend to the people You are sending into my life. You are my help, Father, in my friendships.

Jesus is my best friend. He is a real friend who is more loyal than a brother. He defined the standard when He said in John 15:13 that there is no greater love than to lay down one's life for his friends.

Thank You, Lord that I can trust You with myself and my need for friends. I praise You that are concerned with everything that concerns me. Hallelujah!

Scripture References

Proverbs 13:20 NIV	1 Corinthians 15:33 CEV
Ephesians 5:20 NIV	James 1:17 NIV
Philippians 2:2,3 NCV	Proverbs 17:17
Proverbs 13:20 NIV	Romans 12:15 CEV
Psalm 84:11 NIV	Proverbs 18:24 NLT
Ecclesiastes 4:9,10 NLT	Psalm 37:4,5 NCV
Proverbs 27:17 CEV	

Tithing

Thank you Father that I have come into the inheritance which You gave me in Christ Jesus. Your mercy is great and You love me very much. Though I was spiritually dead, when I acknowledged Jesus as my Lord, You gave me new life with Christ. I have been saved by Your grace. You rescued me from the kingdom of darkness and transferred me into the Kingdom of Your dear Son.

Jesus, as my Lord and High Priest, I bring the first portion of my income to You and worship the Lord my God with it.

Father, I celebrate because of all the good things that You have given to me and my household. I have obeyed You and done everything You commanded me. Now look down from Your holy dwelling place in heaven and bless me as You said in Your Word. Thank

You Father, in Jesus' name. Amen.

Scripture References

Deuteronomy 26:1, 3 AMP   Hebrews 3:1 NCV

Ephesians 2:4-5 NCV

Deuteronomy 26:10-11, 14-15 NLT

Colossians 1:13 NLT

Relationships

Father, in the name of Jesus, I will not withhold good from those who deserve it when it is in my power to help them. I will give to everyone what I owe them. I will pay my taxes and government fees to those who collect them and I will give respect and honor to those who are in authority.

I will not become tired of helping others, for I will be rewarded when the time is right if I do not give up. So, right now, every time I get the chance, I will work for the benefit of all, starting with the people closest to me in the community of faith. Help me, Father, to be a blessing to all those around me.

I will not argue just to be arguing, but will do my best to live at peace with everyone around me. Thank You, Father, for Your help in living this way. In the name of Jesus, amen.

Scripture References

Proverbs 3:27 NLT   Proverbs 3:30 CEV

Romans 13:7 NLT   Romans 12:18

Galatians 6:9,10 MSG

Finding Favor with Others

Father, in the name of Jesus, You smile

on_____

_____ and are gracious and kind to him/
her. He/she is the head and not the tail, above and not
underneath.

Thank You for favor for _____ who
seeks first Your kingdom and finds delight in good.
Grace (favor) is with _____ who loves
the Lord Jesus with an undying love. He/She gives
favor, honor, and love to others and You pour out on
him/her a spirit of favor until his/her cup runs over.
Crown him/her with glory and honor because he/
she is Your masterpiece, which has been created new
in Christ Jesus. He/she is strong, wise, and blessed by
You.

Give _____ knowledge and
skill in all learning and wisdom. Cause him/her to

find favor, compassion and loving-kindness with
_____ (names). _____ finds
favor in the sight of all who look upon him/her this
day, in the name of Jesus.

I pray that _____ knows the love of
Christ and is filled up with the fullness of God. You are
doing far more beyond all that _____
asks or thinks, because Your mighty power is at work
in him/her.

Thank You, Father, that _____
is well-favored by You and by man, in Jesus' name!
Amen.

Scripture References

Numbers 6:25 NLT

Deuteronomy 28:13 NASB

Matthew 6:33 NCV

Proverbs 11:27 MSG

Ephesians 6:24 NIV

Psalm 8:5 NCV

Ephesians 2:10 NLT

Luke 2:40 WE

Daniel 1:17 AMP

Daniel 1:9 AMP

Luke 6:38 WE

Zechariah 12:10 NIV

Esther 2:15,17 NLT

Ephesians 3:19,20 NASB

Helping Others

Father, in the name of Jesus, I will treat others as I would want to be treated. I want love to be my highest goal! I purpose to make it my aim, my great quest in life.

In the name of Jesus, I will not push my way to the front. I will love others and lend them a helping hand. I purpose to build them up in all ways – spiritually, socially and materially – as I am led by Your Spirit. I desire to imitate you, Father, and encourage others and give them strength.

Father, in the name of Jesus, I will love my enemies and be good to them. I will lend without expecting to get anything back. Then, my reward in heaven will be great! I will be acting as a child of the Most High who is good to people even those who are unthankful and cruel.

Thank You, Father for imprinting Your laws upon my heart and inscribing them on my mind – on my inmost thoughts and understanding. As I would like and desire that men would do to me, I do exactly so to them, in the name of Jesus. Amen.

Scripture References

Luke 6:31 CEV

1 Corinthians 14:1 NLT & AMP

Philippians 2:4 MSG

Romans 15:2 NIV & AMP

Luke 6:35,36 CEV

Luke 6:31 AMP

Hebrews 10:16 AMP

Ephesians 6:10 NIV

1 Thessalonians 5:11 NCV

Ephesians 5:1,2 AMP

Finding a Mate

Introduction

In our ministry we hear from many men and women who desire to be married. If that is your desire, we encourage you to ask the Lord to prepare you for marriage. Submit to God's future plans for your life, and purpose to please Him. Do not make your deliberations without knowing His will, at the expense of your personal spiritual growth and transformation. Going from glory to glory (2 Cor. 3:1 8) is not dependent on having a spouse.

Very often, each partner brings emotional baggage into the marriage relationship. As you prepare for marriage, remember that the anointing that was upon Jesus (Luke 4:1 8,1 9) is within you. This anointing will destroy every yoke of bondage (Isaiah 1 0:27) as God exposes emotional wounds and heals your brokenness.

Knowing the reality of your completeness in Christ Jesus will enable you to enter into a healthy relationship, one in which both you and your future partner will grow together spiritually and in every other area of life. Seeking first the Kingdom of God and His righteousness (Matthew 6:33) and doing those things that are pleasing
in His sight (1 John 3:22) will prepare you to be the person designed by Him to fulfill the role of husband or wife.

This prayer is written for your own growth and benefit.

Prayer

Father, I come to You in the name of Jesus, asking for Your will to be done in my life as I look to You for a marriage partner.

I ask that You prepare me for marriage by bringing my darkest secrets to light and revealing my motives. I submit to Your Word that exposes wounded emotions, walls of denial, emotional isolation, silence or excessive talking, anger, rigidity, or any wall that separates me from healthy relationships and from Your love and grace. The weapons that You have given me to bring my thoughts into agreement with Your Word are different from those that the world uses. These powerful weapons destroy the enemy's strong places.

I know the One in whom I trust and I am sure that He is able to guard what I have entrusted to Him, whether I remain unmarried or married, until the day of His return.

Because I love You, Lord, and because I know that You are always at work for my good, everything that happens to me fits into a pattern for my good. It's all according to Your good plan for me. You have chosen me and You have shared Your glory with me. I am Yours!

I remove anything from my life that would get in the way of the race that is before me. I will never give up. I will always look only to Jesus, the One who began our faith and who makes it perfect. He suffered death on the cross but accepted the shame because of the joy that God put before Him. He is now on God's right side
appealing to God for me!

I will run from the temptations that try to capture young people. With Your help, I will always choose to do the right thing. I choose to be faithful, loving, and peaceful. I will enjoy the companionship of people whose hearts are pure. I will stay away from foolish and ignorant arguments that only lead to trouble. I will be kind to everyone, patient and humble.

Father, more than anything else, I put Your work first and what You want. Then, the other things will be mine as well. I won't worry about tomorrow. It will take care of itself.

I know that I can trust You because You loved me first. Even before You made the world, You loved us and chose us in Christ to be holy and without fault in Your eyes. For in Christ, lives all the fullness of God in a human body so I am complete in my union with You.

I come before You, Father, expressing my desire for a Christian mate. I pray that Your will be done in my life. Now, I will enter into Your rest as I trust in You fully. Amen.

Scripture References

Matthew 6:10 NIV	Matthew 6:33-34 CEV
1 Corinthians 4:5 NLT	1 John 4:19
2 Corinthians 10:4 NCV	Ephesians 1:4 NLT
2 Timothy 1:12 NLT	Colossians 2:9,10 NLT
Romans 8:28-30 CEV	Matthew 6:10 NIV
Hebrews 12:1-3 NCV	Hebrews 4:10
Romans 8:34 NCV	John 14:1
2 Timothy 2:22-25 CEV	

Single Female Trusting God for a Mate

Father, in the name of Jesus, I believe that You are at work in me, energizing and creating in me the power and desire to do Your will for Your good pleasure. You are preparing me to receive my future mate who will provide leadership to me the way You do to Your church, not by being domineering but by cherishing me.

Out of respect for Christ, we will be courteously reverent to one another. Prepare me to understand and support my future husband in ways that show my support for You, the Christ.

Father, I believe because he has been divinely chosen by You, my future mate is full of Your wisdom which is straight-forward, gentle and reasonable, overflowing with mercy and blessings. He speaks the truth in love.

Father, I believe that everything not of You shall be removed from my life. I thank You that every word that You give to me will come true. Father, I praise You for performing Your Word! Amen.

Scripture References

Isaiah 62:5 NCV

Ephesians 5:25

James 3:17 MSG

Proverbs 8:8 NCV

Jeremiah 1:12 MSG

Single Male Trusting God for a Mate

Father, in the name of Jesus, I believe that You are providing a wonderful woman who will understand and support me. I pray that we will walk together with like faith and in agreement. Prepare me to provde leadership to my future wife the way You do to Your church, not by being domineering but by cherishing her.

Father, a wise wife is a gift from the Lord and he who finds a wife finds what is good and receives favor from You.

Father, I have written mercy and truth on the tablets of my heart and bind them about my mind. I will receive favor and good understanding from You and from others.

May Your will be done in my life, even as it is in heaven! Amen!

Scripture References

Ephesians 5:22,23 MSG   Philippians 2:2 MSG

Proverbs 18:22 NIV   Jeremiah 1:12 NLT

Proverbs 19:14

Fulfillment as a Single

Father, I thank You that I can steep my life into Your reality and Your provisions. I do not worry about missing out but know that my everyday human concerns will be met. I thank You that I know You love me and I can trust Your Word.

Everything of You, Lord, gets expressed through Jesus so that I can see and hear You clearly. I don't need a telescope, a microscope or a horoscope to realize the fullness of Christ and the emptiness of the universe without Him. When I come to You, that fullness comes together for me too. Your power extends over everything!

So, because of Jesus, I am complete and Jesus is my Lord. I come before You, Father, desiring a born-again Christian mate. I ask that Your will be done in my life. Now, I enter into Your rest by trusting in You, in the name of Jesus. Amen.

Scripture References

Matthew 6:33 MSG   Hebrews 4:10

Colossians 2:9,10 MSG

Preparing Self for Marriage

Father, sometimes being single can be so lonely and so painful. Seeing people in pairs, laughing and having fun, makes me feel even more alone and different.

Lord, please comfort me in these times. Help me to deal with my feelings and thoughts in an appropriate way. Help me to remember to work hard on myself so that I will be whole and mature when You bring the right person into my life.

Help me to remember that this is a time of preparation for the day when I will be joined to another human being for life. Show me how to be responsible for myself and how to allow others to be responsible for themselves.

Teach me about boundaries - what they are and how to establish them instead of walls. Teach me about love – Your love and how to say what is true and say it with love.

Father, I don't want to hold my future spouse or myself back. Help me to take a good look at myself and at who I am in Christ Jesus. Lead me to the right people- teachers, preachers, counselors, and to things – books, CD's, seminars – anyone and anything You can use to teach me Your ways of being and doing right.

Teach me how to choose the mate You would have for me. I ask You to make me wise and help me see things clearly . Help me to recognize the qualities You would have me look for in a mate.

Father, thank You for revealing to me that the choice of a mate is not to be based only on emotions and feelings, but that You have definite guidelines in Your Word for me to use. I know that when I follow what You tell me to do, I will save myself and others a lot of pain and trouble.

Thank You, Lord, that You know me better than I know myself. You know my situation and You know the qualities that I need in another person to fulfill our destiny, individually and as a couple. I depend on You to protect me from the wrong people, so my plans will succeed.

In Jesus' name I pray, amen.

Scripture References

1 Corinthians 1:34 NIV

Ephesians 4:15 WE

Matthew 6:33 AMP

James 1:5-8 WE

Proverbs 3:26 AMP

Proverbs 16:3 AMP

Compatibility in Marriage

Father, in the name of Jesus, God's love has been poured out in our hearts through the Holy Spirit who has been given to us. Because of this, my spouse and I are learning to never give up and to care more for each other than ourselves. We don't strut or have a swelled head. We don't force ourselves on each other and we aren't always about "me first." We don't fly off the handle and we don't keep score of the sins of each other. We don't revel when one grovels; we take pleasure in the flowering of truth. We put up with anything and trust God always. We always look for the best and never look back but always keep going until the end. Our love never dies.

We are no longer babies. We will not be tossed about like a ship that the waves carry one way and then
another, but we will speak the truth in love and grow

up in every way into Christ. We are kind and loving to each other and forgive each other just as God forgave us in Christ. We imitate God in everything we do because we are His children.

Thank You, Father, that our marriage grows stronger each day because it is founded on Your Word and on Your kind of love. We give you the praise for it all, Father, in the name of Jesus. Amen.

Scripture References

Romans 5:5 AMP

1 Corinthians 13:4-8 AMP

Ephesians 4:14,15,32 NCV

1 Corinthians 14:1

Ephesians 5:1, 2 AMP

Wife's Personal Prayer

In the name of Jesus, I will clothe myself with the beauty that comes from within, the unfading beauty of a gentle and quiet spirit, which is so precious to God. I choose to be a good, loyal wife to my husband and treat him with respect. By God's grace, I will be agreeable, sympathetic, loving, compassionate and humble. I will be a blessing and also receive blessings.

By Your Spirit, I am becoming more and more like You. Your bright glory is shining through me. You are creating a clean heart in me, Lord. I am an honest woman who is a jewel to my husband. I will walk wisely and strengthen my family and not destroy them. Houses and wealth are inherited from parents but a wise wife is a gift from the Lord. Praise You Lord, that You were so rich in kindness and grace that You purchased our freedom with the blood of Your Son and forgave our sins. You have showered Your kindness on us, along with wisdom and understanding.

Holy Spirit, I ask You to help me understand and support my husband in ways that show my support for Christ. Teach me to function so that I preserve my own personality while responding to his desires. We are one flesh, and I realize that this unity of persons that preserves individuality is a mystery, but that is how it is when we are united to Christ. So I will keep on loving my husband and let the miracle keep happening!

Just as my husband gives me all that he owes me, I seek to be fair and will give my husband all that I owe him as his wife.

I am strong and graceful and have no fear of the future. My words are wise and my advice is thoughtful. I take good care of my family and am never lazy. Thank You, Father, that I have the wisdom that comes from You and it is pure, peaceful, gentle and easy to please. This wisdom is always ready to help those who are troubled and to do good for others. It is always fair and honest. Thank You Jesus, for sharing that wonderful wisdom with me to be the best wife that I can possibly be! In Jesus' name, amen.

Scripture References

Matthew 16:19 NKJV	Proverbs 19:14 NCV
Ephesians 1:7,8 NLT	Psalm 51:10 NKJV
Ephesians 5:22-23 MSG	2 Corinthians 3:18 CEV
1 Corinthians 7:2-5 NCV	Proverbs 11:6
Proverbs 31:25-27 CEV	Proverbs 12:4 CEV
James 3:17,18 NCV	Proverbs 14:1 NCV
1 Peter 3:1-5, 8, 9 NLT & MSG	

Excerpts taken from *The Heart of Paul* by Ben Campbell Johnson. Copyright © 1976 by A Great Love, Inc., Toccoa, GA. Husbands, I encourage you to pray this prayer in third person for your wife.

Husband's Personal Prayer

Father, in the beginning Your Word tells us that You provided a helper and companion for man. Now I have found a wife to be my companion and she is my treasure. I have received favor from the Lord. I won't ever forget kindness and truth. I will wear them like a necklace and write them on my heart. Then, I will be respected and please both God and people.

I will say about my wife, "There are many good women, but you are the best!" I will show her respect and praise her in public for all she does for me and our family. I will provide leadership to my wife the way Christ does to His Church, not by being domineering but by cherishing. I will go all out in my love for her, exactly as Christ did for the Church – a love marked by giving, not getting.

In the name of Jesus, I give my wife what is due

her, and I share my personal rights with her. Father, I honor my wife and delight in her. In the new life of God's grace, we are equals. I treat my wife as an equal so that our prayers are not hindered.

Lord, I love to worship You and obey Your teachings. My children will have great power in the land because You bless them. Their houses will be full of wealth and riches and their goodness will continue forever. In the name of Jesus, amen.

Scripture References

Matthew 18:18

Genesis 2:18 MSG

Proverbs 18:22 NLT

Proverbs 3:34 NCV

Psalm 112:1-4 CEV, NCV

Ephesians 5:22,23 MSG

1 Corinthians 7:3-5 NCV

1 Peter 3:7-9 NLT

Proverbs 31:28-31 CEV

Developing Patience

Father, I come to You in the name of Jesus. I enjoy serving You, Lord, and I know You want to grant me what I want. Waiting patiently for a marriage partner has become a challenge – a trial, sometimes leading to temptation. I am asking for Your help in developing patience. I depend on You, Lord, and trust You knowing that You will take care of me. I surrender my desire to be married to You.

By Your grace, I surrender my life- all my desires and all that I am and all that I am not—to You. I give control to the Holy Spirit who produces this kind of fruit in me: love, joy, peace, patience, kindness, goodness, truthfulness, gentleness, and the ability to keep my body under control. I belong to Jesus and I strive to live by the Holy Spirit's leading in every part of my life. In exercising self control, I develop patience and in exercising patience, I develop devotion to You.

When trials and temptations crowd into my life, I won't resent them but will realize that they come to test my faith and to produce in me the quality of endurance. I will let the process go on until that endurance is fully developed so that I may become a person of mature character with the right sort of independence.

Father, give me complete knowledge of Your will and spiritual wisdom and understanding. Then, the way that I live will always honor and please You and my life will produce every kind of good fruit. All the while, I will grow as I learn to know You better and better and I will be strengthened with all Your glorious power so that I will have all the endurance and patience I need. I will be filled with joy, always thanking You, Father.

Father, I remove from my life anything that would get in the way and the sin that so easily holds me back and I run the race that is before me and won't ever give up. I look only to Jesus, the One who began my faith and makes it perfect.

With patience, I am able to withstand the difficult times of anxiety and worry and overcome the fear that I may never be married. I have overcome by the blood of the Lamb and by the word of my testimony.

In Jesus' name, amen.

Scripture References

Psalm 37:4,5 NCV

Colossians 1:9-12 NLT

Hebrews 12:1,2 NCV

2 Peter 1:6 NCV & Phillips

James 1:2-4 Phillips

Galatians 5:22-25 WE

Revelation 12:11

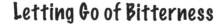
Letting Go of Bitterness

Introduction

In interviews with divorced men and women, I have been encouraged to write a prayer on overcoming bitterness.

Often the injustice of the situation in which these people find themselves creates deep hurts, wounds in the spirit, and anger that is so near the surface that the individuals involved risk sinking into the trap of bitterness and revenge. Their thoughts may turn inward as they consider the unfairness of the situation and dwell on how badly they have been treated. Also, those who suffer abandonment by the parent(s) often harbor bitterness.

In a family divorce situation, bitterness sometimes distorts ideas of what is best for the child/children involved. One parent (and sometimes both parents)

will use the child/children against the other. Unre-
solved anger often moves one marriage partner to
hurt the one he or she holds responsible for the hurt
and sense of betrayal which they feel.

There is healing available. There is a way of escape
for all who will turn to the Healer, obeying Him and
trusting Him.

Prayer

Father, life seems so unjust, so unfair. The pain of
rejection is almost more than I can bear. My past
relationships have ended in strife, anger, rejection and
separation.

Lord, help me to not be bitter or angry or mad. Help
me to never shout or say things to hurt others.

You are the One who has come to free those who
have been treated unfairly. I receive emotional healing by faith, and I thank You for giving me the grace

to stand firm until the process is complete.

Thank You for wise counselors. Thank You for Your Holy Spirit, my Counselor, who comes to show me what is true. Thank You for helping me to work out with fear and trembling what it really means to be saved. You are working in me, creating in my heart the desire and power to do what pleases You.

In the name of Jesus, I forgive those who have wronged me. I choose to live a life of forgiveness because You have forgiven me. With the help of the Holy Spirit, I rid myself of all bitterness, rage, anger, harsh words, and slander. Flood my heart with kindness that I might be tenderhearted and forgiving.

With the help of the Holy Spirit, I will work at living in peace with everyone and work at living a holy life. I purpose to protect others so that no one fails to receive the grace of God. I will watch out that no poisonous root of bitterness grows up to trouble me.

I will watch and pray that I don't enter into temptation or cause others to stumble.

Thank You, Father, that those whom the Son makes free are truly free. I have defeated bitterness and resentment by the blood of the Lamb and Your message.

In Jesus's name, amen.

Scripture References

Ephesians 4:31 NCV	Ephesians 4:31,32 NLT
Luke 4:18 NCV	Hebrews 12:14,15 NLT
Isaiah 10:27	Matthew 26:41
Proverbs 11:14	Romans 14:21
John 15:26 CEV	Jeremiah 1:12 NCV
Philippians 2:12,13 CEV	John 8:36 NCV
Matthew 5:44	Revelation 12:11 CEV

Part III:

Special Prayers

Overcoming Negative Work Attitudes

Thank You, Father, You see the struggle I am having with my employers and fellow-employees. I desire to put off the negative attitudes and put on positive attitudes. I bind mercy, love, discernment and kindness to my mind, and loose all judgments and bad feelings towards others from my mind. I ask You, Holy Spirit, to remind me of godly instruction and my heart will store the commands of my Father. Your words that I've hidden in my heart will enable me to live a long time and provide me with well-being. Thank You for creating in me loyalty and faithfulness. I tie them on my neck and write them deep within my heart. Then I will find favor and approval in Your eyes and in the eyes of my employers and fellow-employees.

God, You are the one who enables me both to want and to actually live out Your good purposes at my

place of employment. I do everything without grumbling and arguing so that I may be blameless and pure, Your
innocent child.

I hear Your Word and do Your Word, not working to make myself look good or flattering people at my workplace, but I act like a slave of Christ, carrying out Your will from my heart. I serve my employer enthusiastically, as though I am serving the Lord, and I know that You will reward every person who does what is right.

I honor You, my Lord, and my work is a sincere expression of my devotion to You, in the name of Jesus. Amen.

Scripture References

Proverbs 3:1-4 CEB

Colossians 3:22-24 NLT

Philippians 2:14,15 NCV

Jeremiah 1:1 2 MSG

Ephesians 6:5-8 CEB

When You Feel Rejected

Introduction

Feelings of rejection and fear of rejection seem to cause an identity crisis. When you are thrown into an identity crisis, you have the opportunity to erase old tapes that have played in your mind for a long time and replace those self-defeating thoughts with God-thoughts.

Your Heavenly Father saw you and approved of you even while you were in your mother's womb (Ps. 139:13-16). He gave you survival tools that would bring you to the place where you are today. He is a Father who has been waiting for you to come home to truth - the truth that will set you free (John 8:32). Jesus came to His own people to bring them life; they rejected Him (John 1:11). He was despised and rejected by men; a man of sorrows who understands your feel-

ings. Jesus bore your sorrow and carried your grief...
the punishment that brings you peace was upon Him
and by His wounds you are healed. (Please read Isaiah
53.)

You were accepted by the Father before the foundation of the world, and there is no higher acceptance
than this! When you see yourself as God's workmanship, as His very own precious child, future rejection
may hurt, but it will be only for a season (1 Peter 1:6.)
The Word of God is your shield against all the fiery
darts of the devil (Eph. 6:16, 17).

For victory over your feeling of rejection, pray the
following prayer in faith and joy.

Prayer

Father, I come before You to bask in Your presence
where I am accepted, and here I find mercy and grace
to help me overcome this fear and feeling of rejection.

Forgive me for being self-conscious rather than God-conscious. You chose me and accepted me before the foundation of the world. I am Your child...valuable and precious in Your sight. When I am facing rejection, I will say, "The LORD is my light and my salvation. Why should I be afraid? The LORD is my fortress...so why should I tremble?" (Psalm 27:1 NLT).

Lord, I know right from wrong and hold Your teaching inside me; I won't pay attention to insults or when people mock me. Thank You for the Holy Spirit who helps me through the process of renewing my mind. I accept myself because You accept me just as I am. So, I will choose not to look at the troubles I see now; rather, I will fix my gaze on things that cannot be seen. For the things that I see now will soon be gone, but the things that I cannot see will last forever.

If with my heart and soul I am doing good, then why would I think I can be stopped? Even if I suffer for it, I am still better off. I won't give the opposition a second thought. Through thick and thin, I will keep my heart at attention, in adoration before Christ, my Master. I will be ready to speak up and tell anyone who asks why I am living the way that I am and always with the utmost courtesy. I will keep a clear conscience before God so that when people throw mud at me, none of it will stick. There is wonderful joy ahead, even though the going is rough for a while down here. These trials are only to test my faith, to see whether it is strong and pure. It is being tested as fire tests gold and purifies it – and my faith is far more precious to You, Lord, than mere gold. So if my faith remains strong after being tried in the test tube of fiery trials, it will bring me much praise and glory and honor on the day of Jesus' return.

Even though I have experienced rejection in this life, I will say that everything You say about me in Your Word is true:

I am blessed with all spiritual blessings in heavenly places in Christ (Eph. 1:3).

I am chosen by You, my Father (Eph. 1:4).

I am Your child according to the good pleasure of Your will (Eph. 1:5).

I am accepted in the Beloved (Eph. 1:6).

I am redeemed through the blood of Jesus (Eph. 1:7).

I am a person of wisdom and revelation in the knowledge of Christ (Eph. 1:17).

I am saved by Your grace (Eph. 2:5).

I am seated in heavenly places in Jesus Christ (Eph. 2:6).

I am Your workmanship (Eph. 2:10).

I am near to You by the blood of Christ (Eph. 2:13).

I am a new creation (Eph. 2:15).

I am of Your household (Eph. 2:19).

I am a citizen of heaven (Eph. 2:19).

I am a partaker of Your promises in Christ
(2 Pet. 1:4).

I am strengthened with might by Your Spirit
(Eph. 3:16).

I allow Christ to dwell in my heart by faith
(Eph. 3:17).

I am rooted and grounded in love (Eph. 3:17).

I speak the truth in love (Eph. 4:15).

I am renewed in the spirit of my mind (Eph. 4:23).

I am Your follower (Eph. 5:1).

I walk in love (Eph. 5:2).

I am light in You (Eph. 5:8).

I walk circumspectly (Eph. 5:15).

I am filled with the Spirit (Eph. 5:18).

I am more than a conqueror (Rom. 8:37).

I am an overcomer (Rev. 12:11).

I am Your righteousness in Christ Jesus (1 Cor. 1:30).

I am healed (1 Pet. 2:24).

I am free (John 8:36).

I am salt (Matt. 5:13).

I am consecrated (1 Cor. 6:11 AMP)

I am sanctified (1 Cor. 6:11).

I am victorious (1 John 5:4).

Everything You say about me is true, Lord.

In Your name I pray, amen.

Scripture References

Hebrews 4:14-16 NLT   Isaiah 51:7,8 MSG

Isaiah 53:3-5 NCV   1 Peter 3:12-17 MSG

2 Corinthians 4:18 NLT   1 Peter 1:6,7 TLB

**For further support, I encourage you to read Psalm 27 and the book of Ephesians in their entirety.

Healthy Lifestyle

Father, I am Your child, belonging only to You. Jesus is Lord over my spirit, soul, and body. Thank you for making me so wonderfully complex. Your workmanship is marvelous—how well I know it.

Lord, thank You for the plans You have for me—plans to prosper me and not to harm me, plans to give me hope and a future. I choose to renew my mind to Your plans for a healthy lifestyle. You have showered your kindness on me, along with all wisdom and understanding. I am sensible and I watch my step. Continue to teach me knowledge and good judgment, for I trust Your commands.

My body is the temple of the Holy Spirit, who lives in me. So here is what I want to do with Your help, Father God. I choose to take my everyday, ordinary life—my sleeping, eating, going-to-work, and walking-around life—and place it before You as an offering. Embracing what You do for me is the best thing I can do for You.

Christ, the Messiah, will be magnified and receive glory and praise in this body of mine and will be boldly exalted in my person.

In Jesus' name, amen.

Scripture References

1 Thessalonians 5:23-24 NCV	Proverbs 14:15 GW
Psalm 139:14 NLT	Psalm 119:66 NIV
Jeremiah 29:11 NIV	1 Corinthians 6:19 NLT
Romans 12:2 NIV	Romans 12:1 MSG
Ephesians 1:8 NLT	Philippians 1:20 AMP

Letting Go of the Past

Father, I realize my helplessness in saving myself, and I honor and praise what Christ Jesus has done for me. I let go of the things I once considered valuable because I'm much better off knowing Jesus Christ my Lord. I throw it all away in order to gain Christ and to have a relationship with Him.

Lord, I have received Your Son, and He has given me the right to become Your child. I unfold my past and put into proper perspective those things that are behind. My old self has been crucified with Christ and I no longer live, but Christ lives in me. I live in this earthly body by faith in the Son of God who loved me and gave Himself for me. I trust in You, Lord, with all my heart and I do not depend on my own understanding. I seek to please You in all I do, and You show me which path to take.

I want to know Christ and experience the power that raised Him from the dead. I want to suffer with Him, even sharing in death so that, one way or another, I will experience the resurrection from the dead! So, whatever it takes, I will be one who lives in the fresh newness of life of those who are alive from the dead.

I don't mean to say that I am perfect. I haven't learned all I should, but I keep working toward that day when I will finally be all that Christ saved me for and wants me to be.

I am bringing all my energies to bear on this one thing: Regardless of my past, I look forward to what lies ahead. I strain to reach the end of the race and receive the prize for which You are calling me up to heaven because of what Christ Jesus did for me.

In Jesus' name I pray, amen.

Scripture References

Proverbs 3:5-6 NLT   John 1:1 2 NIV

Psalm 32:5 AMP   Romans 6:4 TLB

Philippians 3:1 3 NLT   Galatians 2:20 NIV

Philippians 3:1 2-1 4 TLB

Philippians 3:7-9 GW

Philippians 3:1 0-1 1 NLT

When I Feel Afraid

Father, when I am afraid, I will trust in You. I praise You for Your Word. I trust you, God, so I resist fear and renounce fear of man. What can human beings do to me?

Thank You for giving me a spirit of power and of love and of a sound mind. Because of this, I am not ashamed of the testimony of my Lord. I have not received a spirit that makes me a fearful slave. I acknowledge Your Spirit that I received when You adopted me as Your own child. Now, I can call you, "Abba Father."

Jesus, You rescued me by Your death. Because You embraced death and took it upon Yourself, You destroyed the devil's hold on death and freed me from cowering in life, being scared to death of death. I receive the gift that You gave me – peace! You give me Your own peace. This is not like when the people of the world say "peace" to me. You say it differently. You tell me not to fear and not to let anything trouble my heart. I receive this gift because I believe in You, God.

Lord, You are my light and the One who saves me. Why should I fear anyone? You protect my life from danger so why should I tremble? Evil people may try to destroy me. My enemies and those who hate me attack me, but they are defeated. Even if an army surrounds me, I will not be afraid. If I am attacked, I will trust in You, Lord.

Thank You, Holy Spirit, for bringing these things to my remembrance when I am tempted to be afraid. I will trust in my God. In the name of Jesus I pray, amen.

Scripture References

Psalm 56:3 NCV

Hebrews 2:15 MSG

2 Timothy 1:7,8 NKJV

John 14:1,27 NLT

Romans 8:15 NLT

Psalm 27:1-3 NCV

Moving to a New Location

Father, Your Word says that You will work out Your plans for my life. Your faithful love endures forever. I bring to You my apprehensions concerning relocation. I ask that You go before me and my family to level the mountains in finding a new home.

Give my spouse and me wisdom to make wise decisions in choosing the movers and packers best suited to handle our possessions. You cause us to find favor and earn a good reputation with You and people – with the utility companies, with the school systems, and with the banks – with everyone involved in this move.

Father, thank You for giving us (my spouse, children and me) new friends that You would want us to have. We are trusting You to lead us to a church where we can worship together with other believers.

Lord, we depend on You for this move, knowing that You are our Provider. We enjoy serving You and know that You will give us what we desire.

I cast all these cares and concerns on You without fretting or worrying. We offer thanksgiving for this sense of God's wholeness, everything coming together for good will come and settle our minds. You are keeping us in perfect peace because our thoughts are fixed on You!

I trust in You, Lord, with all of my heart. I'm not depending on my own understanding. I will remember You in all I do and know that You will give me success.

Thank You, Father, for Your blessing on this move.

Scripture References

Psalm 138:8 NLT   Psalm 96:1

Isaiah 45:2 NIV

James 1:5

Proverbs 3:4 NLT

Hebrews 10:25

Isaiah 26:3 NLT

Psalm 98:1

Psalm 149:1

Psalm 37:4,5 NCV

Philippians 4:6,7 MSG

Proverbs 3:5,6

When I Feel Hopeless

Father, I come asking You to hear my prayer. Listen, O God, and do not ignore my cry for help! Please listen and answer me, for I am overwhelmed by my troubles. I am scared and shaking and terror grips me.

I wish I had wings like a dove! Then I would fly away and rest. How quickly I would escape, far away from the wind and storm.

I call out to You God, and I know You will rescue me. You redeem my life in peace from this battle of hopelessness that has come against me. I pile my troubles on Your shoulders and thank You for carrying my load and helping me out. Hopelessness lies in wait to swallow me up or trample me all day long. Whenever I am afraid, I choose to have confidence and put my trust and reliance in You. By Your help, God, I praise Your Word. On You I lean, put my trust; I do not entertain fear.

You keep track of all my sorrows. You have collected all my tears in Your bottle. You have recorded each one in Your book. Now I'm thanking You with all my heart. You pulled me from the brink of death, my feet from the cliff edge of doom. Now I stroll at leisure with You in the sunlit fields of life.

I am confident I will see Your goodness while I am here in the land of the living. I wait patiently for You, Lord. I am brave and courageous. Yes, I am waiting patiently.

Father, I give You all my worries and cares, for You care about me. I am well-balanced and cautious—alert, watching out for attacks from Satan, my great enemy. I am standing firm and strong in faith remembering that other Christians all around the world are going through the same kind of sufferings.

In the name of Jesus, I gain the victory by the blood of the Lamb and by the word of my witness. Amen.

Scripture References

Hebrews 4:16 NIV

Psalm 55:1 MSG

Psalm 55:1-2 NLT

Psalm 55:5-8 NCV

Psalm 55:16 CEB

Psalm 55:18 AMP

Psalm 55:22 MSG

Psalm 56:2-4 AMP

Psalm 56:8 NLT

Psalm 56:13 MSG

Psalm 27:13-14 NLT

1 Peter 5:7 NLT

1 Peter 5:8 AMP

1 Peter 5:8-9 NLT

Revelation 12:11 CEB

About the Author:

Germaine Griffin Copeland, founder and president of Word Ministries, Inc., is the author of the *Prayers That Avail Much*® **books,** *A Global Call to Prayer* **and** other publications. Her writings provide scriptural prayer instructions that will help you pray more effectively.

Word Ministries, Inc. is a prayer and teaching ministry whose vision is to unite followers of Jesus for the purpose of praying *Prayers That Avail Much*®. Through her writings and multiple prayers, they are equipping believers to be more effective intercessors and fruitful workers in God's Vineyard. Germaine is training other prayer leaders in the First Fruit Prayer Groups that meet during the first week of each month with a common agenda. As more prayer groups are added, the company of intercessors is marching across the land, even to other countries.

On the website, www.prayers.org, you can sign up to be a member of the Global Company of Intercessors and receive bi-monthly prayer assignments. You may also subscribe to the Daily Prayers. We are praying for the nations, for God's will to be done on every continent.

Germaine is the daughter of the late Reverend A. H. "Buck" and Donnis Brock Griffin. She and her husband, Everette, have four children, eleven grandchildren and their prayer assignments increase as great-grandchildren are born into the family. Germaine and Everette reside in Greensboro, Georgia, on beautiful Lake Oconee.

Mission Statement:

Word Ministries, Inc.

Equipping the body of Christ to be effectual Intercessors and fruitful Workers in the Vineyard.

You may contact Word Ministries by writing:

Word Ministries, Inc.

P. O. Box 289

Good Hope, Georgia 30641

-or calling-

770.267.7603

www.prayers.org

Please include your testimonies and

praise reports when you write.

Other Books by Germaine Copeland:

A Global Call to Prayer

Prayers That Avail Much Commemorative Gift Edition

Prayers That Avail Much Commemorative
Leather Edition

Prayers That Avail Much for the Workplace

Prayers That Avail Much Volume 1

Prayers That Avail Much Volume 1 Mass Market Edition

Prayers That Avail Much Volume 2

Prayers That Avail Much Volume 3

Prayers That Avail Much for Men — pocket edition

Prayers That Avail Much for Women — pocket edition

Prayers That Avail Much for Mothers — paperback

Prayers That Avail Much for Moms — pocket edition

Prayers That Avail Much for Teens

Prayers That Avail for the College Years

Prayers That Avail Much Gold Letter Edition

Prayers That Avail Much Gold Letter Gift Edition

PRAYER OF SALVATION

God loves you—no matter who you are, no matter what your past. God loves you so much that He gave His one and only begotten Son for you. The Bible tells us that "...whoever believes in Him shall not perish but have eternal life" (John 3:16 NIV). Jesus laid down His life and rose again so that we could spend eternity with Him in heaven and experience His absolute best on earth. If you would like to receive Jesus into your life, say the following prayer out loud and mean it from your heart.

Heavenly Father, I come to You admitting that I am a sinner. Right now, I choose to turn away from sin, and I ask You to cleanse me of all unrighteousness. I believe that Your Son, Jesus, died on the cross to take away my sins. I also believe that He rose again from the dead so that I might be forgiven of my sins and made righteous through faith in Him. I call upon the name of Jesus Christ to be the Savior and Lord of my life. Jesus, I choose to follow You and ask that You fill me with the power of the Holy Spirit. I declare that right now I am a child of God. I am free from sin and full of the righteousness of God. I am saved in Jesus' name. Amen.

If you prayed this prayer to receive Jesus Christ as your Savior for the first time, please contact us on the Web at **www.harrisonhouse.com** to receive a free book.

Or you may write to us at

Harrison House • P.O. Box 35035 • Tulsa, Oklahoma 74153

Fast. Easy.
Convenient.

For the latest Harrison House product information
and author news, look no further than your computer.
All the details on our powerful, life-changing products
are just a click away. New releases, E-mail subscriptions,
Podcasts, testimonies, monthly specials—find it all in
one place. Visit harrisonhouse.com today!

harrisonhouse

The Harrison House Vision

Proclaiming the truth and the power

Of the Gospel of Jesus Christ

With excellence;

Challenging Christians to

Live victoriously,

Grow spiritually,

Know God intimately.

Made in the USA
Columbia, SC
18 March 2022